Pigs

Pigs

Peter Murray

T H E C H I L D ' S W O R L D®, INC.

Library of Congress Cataloging-in-Publication Data
Murray, Peter, 1952 Sept. 29-
Pigs/written by Peter Murray.
p.   cm.
Includes index.
Summary: Introduces the physical characteristics, behavior and life cycle of pigs.
ISBN 1-56766-378-8 (alk. paper)
1. Swine—Juvenile literature. 2. Suidae—Juvenile Literature.
[1. Pigs.] I. Title.
SF395.5.M87 1997
636.4—dc21   97-8363
CIP
AC

Photo Credits

Andy Sacks/Tony Stone Worldwide: 10
Art Wolfe/Tony Stone Images: 23
ANIMALS ANIMALS: Robert Maier: 15, 16
Bill Lea/DEMBINSKY PHOTO ASSOC: 24
COMSTOCK, Inc: 9
Jack Daniels/Tony Stone Images: 2
Kevin Horan/Tony Stone Images: 26
Larime Photos: DEMBINSKY PHOTO ASSOC: 6
Peter Cade/Tony Stone Images: 30
Photri, Inc.: cover
Renee Lynn/Tony Stone Images: 19
Stan Osolinski/DEMBINSKY PHOTO ASSOC: 20
Tony Stone Worldwide: 13, 29
William Muñoz: cover

On the cover...

Front cover: This pig is eating in a barn.
Page 2: This *Middle White pig* is raising its snout to smell.

Table of Contents

There are always many things to see on a farm. Out in the meadow, cows and horses eat green grass. By the pond, ducks and geese waddle into the water. And over by the barn, a few creatures grunt and roll in the mud. They make sounds such as "Oink!" and "Snort!" What could these strange animals be? Pigs!

These farm pigs are walking in the mud.

What Do Pigs Look Like?

Pigs are also called **hogs**. They have a thick body with a round nose, or **snout**, at one end and a curly tail at the other. They also have teeth that can grow into sharp **tusks**. People who raise pigs usually clip the tusks to make them less dangerous.

A pig's skin is thick and covered with bristly hair. When people get hot, they perspire. When pigs get hot, they roll in the mud. They don't do it because they like to be dirty. They are just trying to stay cool.

This pig is cooling off from the hot sun.

Most farm-raised pigs give birth to 8 to 12 babies at a time. The babies are called **piglets**. A piglet weighs about two pounds when it is born. The mother pig, called a **sow**, nurses her babies with milk from her body. The baby pigs grow quickly. In eight months they are old enough to have their own babies!

Wild pigs only have babies once a year. They usually have five or six babies at a time. Wild piglets are striped when they are young. When they grow up, they have shaggy dark hair like their parents.

These *Yorkshire piglets* are staying close together.

What Do Pigs Eat?

Pigs will eat almost anything. Wild pigs eat nuts, fruits, leaves, and grains. They use their powerful snouts to dig for tasty roots and bulbs. They eat insects, worms, and small animals if they can catch them. If they find a dead animal, they will eat that, too!

On farms, pigs are usually fed corn, oats, and other grains. They also eat meal made from soybeans, meat scraps, milk, and other high-protein foods. When a pig gets all the food it wants, it grows fast. In 1933, a huge hog named Big Bill weighed 2,552 pounds. That's over a ton!

These farm pigs are eating grains.

Are Pigs Very Smart?

Pigs are one of the smartest farm animals. They are as smart as most dogs. Pigs have a good memory and learn tricks easily. They can be taught to fetch, just like a dog. Pigs have very sensitive noses. In Europe, they are trained to sniff out underground mushrooms called *truffles*. Police have also used them to search for buried drugs and explosives.

Because pigs can be trained easily, some people keep them as pets. A miniature pig called the *Vietnamese potbellied pig* is sometimes sold in pet shops. It is only 14 inches tall and weighs about 40 pounds.

Vietnamese potbellied pigs like this one are much smaller than farm pigs.

All male pigs are called **boars**. But wild pigs, both male and female, are called boars, too. Ten thousand years ago, all pigs were wild. A pig called the *Eurasian wild boar* was the ancestor of our farm pigs. A few wild boars still live in the forests of Asia and Europe. Wild boars are ferocious fighters when they are cornered. They are fast and powerful and their tusks are razor-sharp. A full-grown male can weigh more than 400 pounds.

This *wild boar* lives in a forest in Germany.

Wild boars called *razorbacks* live in the southeastern United States. Razorbacks are the relatives of farm pigs that escaped long ago. They look and act much like their wild ancestors.

Other kinds of wild pigs live in Africa and Asia. The *giant forest hog* of Africa is the largest wild pig. It is six feet long and can weigh up to 600 pounds. A smaller species called the *bush pig* lives in Africa and on the island of Madagascar.

This *giant forest hog* has sharp tusks.

African warthogs live on the wide-open plains of Africa. They are called warthogs because they have a wartlike lump under each eye. Male warthogs' sharp tusks can grow up to two feet long! Warthogs are the only wild pigs that live in the open. All of the others live in jungles or forests.

This *African warthog* is getting a drink of water.

Are Wild Pigs In Danger?

One of the oddest-looking members of the pig family is the *babirusa*. The babirusa is a four-tusked wild pig of Indonesia. The babirusa's upper teeth grow up through its snout and curve over its forehead. The bottom teeth curve up on each side of its jaw. Babirusa are expert swimmers. They are found only in the dense jungles of Sulawesi and the Molucca Islands. Babirusa are **endangered**, which means that they are in danger of dying out. Only a few thousand remain alive.

This *babirusa* is caked with mud.

Do Pigs Have Any Relatives?

Small piglike animals called *peccaries* or *javelina* live wild in parts of North and South America. They look and act like small wild pigs. They have a piglike snout and small, sharp tusks. Peccaries are related to the wild pigs of Africa and Eurasia. But even though they may look a lot like pigs, peccaries are not true members of the pig animal family.

Peccaries are found from the southwestern United States to Argentina. They travel in small family groups. Like their relative the pigs, peccaries will eat almost anything. One of their favorite foods is the prickly pear cactus.

Peccaries like this one look a lot like pigs.

What Are Pigs Used For?

Today, more than 860 million hogs live on farms all over the world. Most farmers raise their pigs to be used for meat. Pig meat, called **pork**, is used to make ham, bacon, and pork chops. Spareribs, bologna, bratwurst, and salami are all made from pork, too.

Many pigs are also raised for their skins. Pigskin is used to make a material called **leather**. Belts, shoes, and gloves can all be made from leather. Many footballs are also made from pigskin leather.

This piglet is standing inside a barn.

Pigs are used for other things, too. Their stiff hairs are used to make bristles for brushes. Pig bristles are also used for stuffing mattresses and baseball gloves. Drug companies use pigs to make insulin and other medicines. And sometimes, the fat from pigs is used to make shaving cream, soap, and candles.

Some pigs are used for medical research. Pigs don't look or act much like human beings, but many of their organs are very much like ours. Scientists use pigs to test new drugs. They use pigs to study heart disease, alcoholism, and diabetes. They even put pigs on treadmills to find out whether exercise makes them healthier.

This pig is chewing on the wall of its pen.

Pigs have been raised by humans for nearly ten thousand years, and today they are more important than ever. They are raised a few at a time on small family farms, and by the thousands on huge modern farms. They are running on treadmills to help medical science. They are our pets and our truffle-hunters. They are even starring in some movies!

This little piglet is eating a snack.

Glossary

boar (BOR)
Male pigs are called boars. Wild pigs are called boars, too.

endangered (en–DANE–jerd)
When an animal is endangered, it is in danger of dying out. Some kinds of wild pigs are endangered.

hog (HOGG)
Hog is another name for a pig.

leather (LEH–thur)
Leather is a material made from the skin of animals. Pigskin leather is used to make shoes, gloves, and footballs.

piglets (PIG–lets)
Piglets are baby pigs. Piglets only weight about two pounds when they are born.

pork (PORK)
Pork is another word for pig meat.

snout (SNOWT)
A snout is a pig's nose. Pigs use their snouts in many ways.

sow (SOW)
A sow is a female pig.

tusks (TUSSKS)
Tusks are teeth that grow very long and sharp. Farmers usually clip the pigs' tusks to make them less dangerous.

Index